The Impact of the Trump Administration's Indo-Pacific Strategy on Regional Economic Governance

Policy Studies

an East-West Center series

Description

Policy Studies presents original research on pressing economic and political policy challenges for governments and industry across Asia, and for the region's relations with the United States. Written for the policy and business communities, academics, journalists, and the informed public, the peer-reviewed publications in this series provide new policy insights and perspectives based on extensive fieldwork and rigorous scholarship.

EastWestCenter.org/PolicyStudies

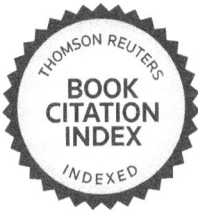

Policy Studies is indexed in the *Web of Science Book Citation Index*. The *Web of Science* is the largest and most comprehensive citation index available.

Notes to Contributors

Submissions may take the form of a proposal or complete manuscript. Please send to: Publications@EastWestCenter.org.

East-West Center
1601 East-West Road
Honolulu, Hawai'i 96848-1601
Tel: 808.944.7197

Policy
Studies | 79

The Impact of the Trump Administration's Indo-Pacific Strategy on Regional Economic Governance

Kaewkamol Karen Pitakdumrongkit

The Impact of the Trump Administration's Indo-Pacific Strategy on Regional Economic Governance
Kaewkamol Karen Pitakdumrongkit

ISSN 1547-1349 (print) and 1547-1330 (electronic)
ISBN 978-0-86638-287-8 (print) and 978-0-86638-286-1 (electronic)

Print copies are available from Amazon.com. Free electronic copies of most titles are available on the East-West Center website, at EastWestCenter.org/PolicyStudies, where submission guidelines can also be found. Questions about the series should be directed to:

Publications Office
East-West Center
1601 East-West Road
Honolulu, Hawai'i 96848-1601

Telephone: 808.944.7197

Publications@EastWestCenter.org
EastWestCenter.org/PolicyStudies

Contents

List of Acronyms

ACIA	ASEAN Comprehensive Investment Agreement
AEC 2025	ASEAN Economic Community Blueprint 2025
AANZFTA	ASEAN-Australia-New Zealand FTA
ACFTA	ASEAN-China FTA
AIFTA	ASEAN-India FTA
AJCEP	ASEAN-Japan Comprehensive Economic Partnership
AKFTA	ASEAN-Korea FTA
ASW	ASEAN Single Window
APEC	Asia-Pacific Economic Cooperation
ABMI	Asian Bond Markets Initiative
ADB	Asian Development Bank
ADBI	Asian Development Bank Institute
AIIB	Asian Infrastructure Investment Bank
ATTN	Asian Think Tanks Network
ASEAN	Association of Southeast Asian Nations
BCIM	Bangladesh-China-India-Myanmar
BIMSTEC	Bay of Bengal Initiative for Multi-Sectoral Technical and Economic Cooperation

BRI	Belt Road Initiative
BUILD Act	Better Utilization of Investments Leading to Development Act of 2018
CLMV	Cambodia, Laos, Myanmar, and Vietnam
CSIS	Center for Strategic and International Studies
CFIUS	Committee on Foreign Investment in the United States
CPTPP	Comprehensive and Progressive Agreement for Trans-Pacific Partnership
IORA	Indian Ocean Rim Association
IAI	Initiative for ASEAN Integration
IIAs	International investment agreements
ISDS	Investor-state dispute settlement
FIRRMA	Foreign Investment Risk Review Modernization Act of 2018
GSP	Generalized System of Preferences
GMS	Greater Mekong Subregion
NEAT	Network of East Asian Think-Tanks
NAFTA	North American Free Trade Agreement
USTR	Office of the United States Trade Representative
OPIC	Overseas Private Investment Corporation
RCEP	Regional Comprehensive and Economic Partnership
TPP	Trans-Pacific Partnership
UNCTAD	United Nations Conference on Trade and Development
IDFC	U.S. International Development Finance Corporation
KORUS FTA	U.S.-Korea FTA

Executive Summary

During his visit to Asia in November 2017, U.S. President Donald Trump unveiled his vision of a "Free and Open Indo-Pacific" as the U.S. approach to Asia. Secretary of State Mike Pompeo elaborated on the administration's Indo-Pacific strategy at the Indo-Pacific Business Forum of the U.S. Chamber of Commerce in Washington, D.C., on July 30, 2018. He announced that $113 million will be allocated as a "down payment" to fund new initiatives to bolster the digital economy, energy, and infrastructure of the region. Pompeo also pledged to strengthen American support for key regional institutions such as the Association of Southeast Asian Nations (ASEAN), Asia-Pacific Economic Cooperation (APEC), Lower Mekong Initiative, and Indian Ocean Rim Association (IORA) to advance the Indo-Pacific strategy (Pompeo 2018). Moreover, speaking at the APEC CEO Summit in November 2018 in Papua New Guinea, Vice President Mike Pence discussed the strategy's economic components. Regarding trade, Pence echoed Trump's 2017 APEC speech that Washington will "make bilateral trade agreements with any Indo-Pacific nation that wants to be our partner and that will abide by the principles of fair and reciprocal trade." The United States also seeks to promote

> *During his visit to Asia in November 2017, U.S. President Donald Trump unveiled his vision of a 'Free and Open Indo-Pacific' as the U.S. approach to Asia*

private sector investment. Moreover, Pence stressed that the Trump administration aims to assist regional states on sustainable infrastructure development (Pence 2018).

The Impact of the Trump Administration's Indo-Pacific Strategy on Regional Economic Governance

Overview

This paper examines the economic aspects of the Trump administration's Indo-Pacific strategy. "Strategy" is defined as "the collection of plans and policies that comprise the state's deliberate effort to harness political, military, diplomatic, and economic tools together to advance that state's national interest" (Feaver 2009). In other words, this paper scrutinizes the economic components of the U.S. Indo-Pacific strategy and its impact on the future development of Asian economic governance. The paper focuses on the following questions: What are the economic

The Trump administration's Indo-Pacific strategy is limited to trade, investment, and infrastructure development

components of America's Indo-Pacific strategy? How has this policy been received by regional states? How will Indo-Pacific and Asia Pacific policies interact to shape the future development of Asian economic architectures? What should American and regional policymakers do to prevent or lessen conflicts among their different policies and strategies and further foster economic regionalism?

The Trump administration's Indo-Pacific strategy is limited to trade, investment, and infrastructure development, and the level of reception by regional states varies by issue area, with infrastructure and investment being positively received, and trade being negatively received. While there is no obvious conflict between Indo-Pacific and Asia Pacific investment and infrastructure development policies, both the United States and Asian nations have practiced mutual neglect, which will result in more fragmented governance architectures. A "governance architecture" refers to the overarching structure of public and private institutions comprising organizations, principles, norms, regulations, and decision-making procedures in a given issue area of international relations (Biermann et al. 2009, 15). To alleviate policy clashes and lessen the "noodle bowl" effect of overlapping rules and regulations, this paper suggests that American and Asian governments should: (1) immediately pursue collaboration in the areas of investment and infrastructure; (2) advance investment cooperation via capacity training and investment treaty consolidation; (3) enhance infrastructure collaboration via the Better Utilization of Investments Leading to Development Act of 2018 (or BUILD Act of 2018), joint ventures, public-private partnership, and capacity training; (4) push forward trade cooperation via formal and Track 2 (informal networks) dialogue into a policymaking process; and (5) encourage more inter-bloc dialogue.

This paper is organized as follows. The beginning section discusses a brief history of the U.S. Indo-Pacific strategy. The economic elements of the policy are then unpacked, followed by the reception of the regional states to the strategy. Next, interplay between the agendas and policies of the United States and regional players concerning regional economic governance architectures is examined. The paper then provides policy recommendations for the United States and Indo-Pacific participants to enhance economic collaboration.

Backdrop: Rivalry with China

The Indo-Pacific as an idea of strategic thinking is not new. It was coined by Gurpreet Khurana in his 2007 Strategic Analysis article "Security of Sea Lines: Prospects for India–Japan Cooperation." In his piece, the term was used to refer to two strategic and political spaces encompassed by the Indian and Pacific Oceans. This conceptualization has long been familiar to those in the American policymaking circle. For instance, the U.S. Department of Defense's Indo-Pacific Command (previously named Pacific Command) ·has operated across two bodies of water as a single interconnected geostrategic plane. Also, the notions of "Free" and "Open" echo the spirit of APEC, of which the United States is a member. Illustratively, at the 1993 APEC Ministerial Meeting in Seattle, Washington, APEC participants pledged to continuously contribute to "an expanding world economy and [to support] an open international trading system…[and] reduce trade and investment barriers so that… trade expands within the region and with the world and goods, services, capital and investment flow freely among [regional] economies" (APEC 1993). Likewise, at the following year's ministerial meeting in Bogor, Indonesia, these economies agreed to "adopt the long-term goal of free and open trade and investment in the Asia-Pacific [which] will be pursued promptly by further reducing barriers to trade and investment and by promoting the free flow of goods, services and capital among [the] economies" (APEC 1994).

At the 1993 APEC Ministerial Meeting in Seattle, participants pledged to contribute to an expanding world economy

Furthermore, President Obama's administration leaned on the Indo-Pacific concept to emphasize India as "a major pillar" of its Asia policy. Such recognition of New Delhi as one of the key regional players contributed to soaring U.S.-India ties under his presidency.[1] The upgrade of an annual strategic dialogue to a strategic and commercial dialogue in 2015 as a platform to discuss bilateral relations at the highest political level was a case in point (Mistry 2016).

While Washington has relied on the term "Indo-Pacific" to conceptualize the region and formulate its foreign policies, the Trump administration's use of the term has departed from previous eras. His administration is the first to use the term in a national document such as the *2017 National Security Strategy* (*NSS*), and his Indo-Pacific policy was crafted in light of a rising and revisionist China (Grossman 2018). The policy was formulated based on an assumption that China and the United States are locked in a power contestation.

What motivates the Trump administration to coin and pursue the Indo-Pacific strategy amid the U.S.-China rivalry backdrop? The first motivation concerns the U.S.-China rivalry itself. President Trump's cabinet views the United States and China as being in strategic competition in the Indo-Pacific region, and if the contestation is not well managed, it could jeopardize U.S. interests.[2] National documents cast Beijing as a revisionist power. For example, the 2018 National Defence Strategy (NDS) contends that "China is leveraging military modernization, influence operations, and predatory economics to coerce neighboring countries to reorder the Indo-Pacific region to their advantage" (NDS 2018, 2). Likewise, the *NSS* conveys that "China seeks to displace the United States in the Indo-Pacific region, expand the reaches of its state-driven economic model, and reorder the region in its favor" (*NSS* 2017, 25).

Trump's cabinet views the United States and China as being in in strategic competition in the Indo-Pacific region; if not well managed, it could jeopardize U.S. interests

Moreover, Washington is specifically concerned with Beijing's economic diplomacy, namely the latter's policy combination of inducements and coercion to shape foreign policy behaviors of particular regional stakeholders. As the *NSS* highlights, Beijing "is using economic inducements and penalties, influence operations, and implied military threats to persuade other states to heed its political and security agenda. China's infrastructure investments and trade strategies reinforce its geopolitical aspirations." This economic diplomacy partly accounted for Beijing's ability to utilize its economic leverage to gain an upper hand in international relations, as seen in the South

China Sea case (*NSS* 2017, 46). Additionally, Chinese involvement in Myanmar, Bangladesh, and Sri Lanka has been reported to be driven more by geopolitical strategy than economics (Samaranayake 2012). This concern was also reflected in Vice President Mike Pence's remark at the 2018 APEC CEO Summit. While not directly addressing China and the China-led Belt Road Initiative (BRI), Pence stipulated that Washington's approach to infrastructure development is "a better option. We don't drown our partners in a sea of debt. We don't coerce or compromise your independence. The United States deals openly, fairly. We do not offer a constricting belt or a one-way road" (Pence 2018).

China's rising ambition, as evinced by the BRI and Asian Infrastructure Investment Bank (AIIB), has raised anxiety in several governments in the Indo-Pacific region. Announced by Chinese President Xi Jinping in 2013, BRI—comprising the 21st Century Maritime Silk Road and Silk Road Economic Belt—is aimed at augmenting China's connectivity with other countries. At the time of this writing, the plan involves **65 countries**, covers approximately $23 trillion in combined GDP, and includes 4.4 billion people (*Global Times* 2017). Launched in 2014, AIIB is a China-led multilateral development bank purposed to provide financial support to infrastructure projects in Asia. The bank now has 87 members from around the world (AIIB 2018).

The Trump administration perceives the Indo-Pacific as a zone where America's economic future lies

While China-led BRI and AIIB schemes have not yet led to enhanced Chinese power in the region, some countries are nevertheless worried that these initiatives possess great potential to enable Beijing to expand its sphere of influence and increase its maritime power projection.[3] Such apprehension was mentioned in the *NSS*, which argues that "[s]tates throughout the region are calling for sustained U.S. leadership in a collective response that upholds a regional order respectful of sovereignty and independence" (*NSS* 2017, 46). In short, the U.S. Indo-Pacific strategy was coined against this backdrop to assure American partners that Washington is here to work with them to foster a "Free and Open Indo-Pacific."

Another motivation for the new Indo-Pacific strategy is America's recognition of Asia as important to its economy. The Trump administration perceives the Indo-Pacific as a zone where America's economic future lies.[4] Pointedly, it houses the world's most dynamic economies and more than 50 percent of the earth's population; obviously, this can be a very lucrative market for U.S. businesses. Around 60 percent of the global maritime commerce passes through Asia (UNCTAD 2016). According to one analysis, "[t]he Indian Ocean and the Asia Pacific will be at the centre stage of the global container market" in the next two decades (Futurenautics 2013, 76). In the realm of energy, approximately **40 percent of the world's liquefied natural gas trade occurs** in the South China Sea (U.S. EIA 2017).

Economic data has shown that the Asian region is significant to the U.S. economy. In 2017, the two-way trade between America and Asia stood around $1,544 billion (U.S. Census Bureau 2018a). As of July 2018, China, Japan, South Korea, and India were among the top 10 U.S. trading partners, constituting 15.4 percent, 5.1 percent, 3 percent and 2.1 percent of America's trade with the world (U.S. Census Bureau 2018b). In addition, U.S. investment in Asia has grown about 10 percent annually, rising from $227 billion in 2001 to $605 billion in 2011 (East-West Center 2013).

It should be highlighted that America's adoption of the "Indo-Pacific" term inevitably draws attention to the importance of India in the regional economy. A senior White House officer posited that such adoption was partially attributable to the administration's recognition of India's rise (*Channel NewsAsia* 2017). And it's not a surprising move, given the soaring America-India economic ties in recent years. According to the East-West Center's *India Matters for America*, bilateral U.S.-India trade rose from $37 billion in 2007 to $109 billion in 2015. Washington's imports from New Delhi quadrupled from about $11 billion in 2000 to almost $45 billion in 2015 (East-West Center 2017, 9). Additionally, U.S. investment in India increased almost 200 percent over a decade, reaching approximately $28 billion in 2015, while India's foreign direct investment in America amounted to $9.2 billion in 2015, which is a rise of more than 500 percent since 2006 (East-West Center 2017, 12). Moreover, the state not only houses 1.3 billion people, but has 600 million individuals who are under 25 years old. Consequently, India's huge market potential and young workforce combined could make New Delhi one of the key economic players in the Indo-Pacific economy and beyond (Jack 2018). Its economic potential notwithstanding, the country is not a party to APEC. While several experts called for the American backing of India's APEC membership bid, Washington has not yet voiced explicit support for New Delhi's entry into the bloc (Ayres 2017, Gupta 2017).

Additionally, Asian governments have been deepening their economic integration via several schemes, including the *ASEAN Economic Community Blueprint 2025* (*AEC 2025*), Comprehensive and Progressive Agreement for Trans-Pacific Partnership (CPTPP), and Regional Comprehensive and Economic Partnership (RCEP). *AEC 2025* is an integration project among 10 Southeast Asian economies aimed at achieving "a highly integrated and cohesive economy; a competitive, innovative, and dynamic ASEAN; enhanced connectivity and sectoral cooperation; a resilient, inclusive, people-oriented, and people-centred ASEAN; and a global ASEAN" (ASEAN Secretariat 2015). CPTPP is a free trade agreement (FTA) involving 11 Asia Pacific states with the purpose of liberalizing trade and investment in key areas such as technical barriers to trade, sanitary and phytosanitary measures, and state-owned enterprises. The negotiation concluded in January 2018. Once CPTPP is enforced, this bloc will cover a market of 495 million people and have a combined GDP of CA\$13.5 trillion (Government of Canada 2018). RCEP is an FTA under negotiation among 10 Southeast Asian countries and six of ASEAN's dialogue partners. It is aimed at merging the existing ASEAN-Plus-One FTAs into a single contract. Talks are expected to be finished by the end of 2019 (*The Japan Times* 2018a). If concluded, this mega-trade deal will cover 46 percent of the global population and 24 percent of the world's GDP (Jozuka 2017). Being more integrated economically, the significance of the Indo-Pacific region to U.S. businesses will heighten in years to come.

However, this area has several choke points that risk jeopardizing freedom of navigation, a principle that Washington holds dearly (Green and Shearer 2012). Consequently, the Indo-Pacific strategy was crafted to safeguard current and future U.S. commercial stakes in the region.[5] Additionally, this policy was driven by Washington's realization that it needs to convince its regional partners to beef up their responsibilities in fostering regional stability. For example, this strategy regards India as a potential stabilizing actor on security and economic fronts. As some scholars claim, this shows that the Trump administration is conducting Jacksonian foreign policy, which requires more burden-sharing by allies. In short, the Indo-Pacific strategy calls for the players that the United States promises to defend to do their parts or meet their obligations (Clarke and Ricketts 2017; Hanson 2017).

1. The Economic Components of the U.S. Indo-Pacific Strategy

The U.S. envisions a "Free and Open Indo-Pacific" as "a region where sovereign and independent nations and diverse cultures can all prosper side-by-side, and thrive in freedom and in peace" (Douglas 2018). The policy hinges on two modifiers: "Free" and "Open." Here, "free" means freedom from coercion by other players, entailing the concepts of sovereignty, rules-based order, and dispute settlement. "Open" refers to open commons (e.g., sea lanes, airways, cyberspace), open logistics (e.g., connectivity that drives regional growth and integration), open investment (e.g., investment environment fostering market economics), and open trade (e.g., free, fair, reciprocal trade). This strategy is also inclusive as Washington welcomes other like-minded countries to join forces in enhancing the Free and Open region.

Economics is seen as key to the Trump administration strategy, as it puts more emphasis on economic matters than other administrations.[6] This is evident in the *NSS* positing that "economic security is the U.S. national security" (*NSS* 2017, 17). In December 2017, President Trump stressed that "[e]conomic vitality, growth and prosperity at home is absolutely necessary for American power and influence abroad" (Trump 2017a). To delineate this point, the administration believes that economic gains allow a state to bolster its security. A strong and prosperous U.S. economy provides Washington with resources to augment its military capabilities and its ability to project power internationally. As a result, Washington will tailor its "approaches to different regions of the world to protect U.S. national interests" (*NSS* 2017, 45). The U.S. policy in the Indo-Pacific is no exception. Regarding the direction of regional U.S. economic engagement, the *NSS* suggests an overarching theme of creating good regional economic governance. The text indicates that Washington

> will encourage regional cooperation to maintain free and open seaways, transparent infrastructure financing practices, unimpeded commerce, and the peaceful resolution of disputes…pursue bilateral trade agreements on a fair and reciprocal basis…seek equal and reliable access for American exports…work with partners to build a network of states dedicated to free markets and protected from forces that would subvert their [sovereignty and] strengthen cooperation with allies on high-quality infrastructure" (*NSS* 2017, 47).

More detailed policy directions can be teased out from Deputy Assistant Secretary Alex Wong's press briefing in April 2018, which unveiled Washington's plans to collaborate with regional participants in three economic areas: trade, investment, and infrastructure/connectivity. On trade, the administration aims at fostering "free, fair, and reciprocal" trade by lowering barriers.[7] To America, the principles of "fairness" and "reciprocity" serve as a basis for open trade and the upholding of contracts, and Washington wants to promote these principles to redress its trade deficit issue partially caused by tariffs and nontariff barriers of Asian nations.[8] Moreover, Trump's *2018 Trade Policy Agenda and 2017 Annual Report* submitted to Congress in March 2018 further elaborates on how the administration would promote such "free, fair, and reciprocal" trade. The report stressed that the trade policy rests on five major pillars, with two of them having international aspects: negotiating better international deals, and reforming the multilateral trading system.

Regarding the former, Washington has struck deals with other economies that are more favorable to its workers and businesses, e.g., improving existing FTAs, namely the United States-Mexico-Canada Agreement (formerly known as the North American Free Trade Agreement (NAFTA)) and the U.S.-Korea FTA (KORUS FTA). As for the parties to the Trans-Pacific Partnership (TPP)—a mega-trade deal the United States withdrew from in January 2017—which do not have bilateral trade contracts with Washington, the administration "will continue efforts to build stronger, better, and fairer trading relationships with these countries" (USTR 2018, 12). Regarding multilateral trading system reform, the administration desires to make the system work better in ways that can more effectively safeguard American interests. The report also connotes America's willingness to work with like-minded participants to build global trade systems that increase the standard of living for both U.S. citizens and the world at large.

In the region, Washington wants to boost the investment climate, enhance private sector participation, and encourage entrepreneurship and innovation

On investment, Washington wants to boost the investment climate, enhance private sector participation, and ensure that investment in the region encourages entrepreneurship and innovation. Wong remarked that the United States is supporting "more open investment environments [and] more transparent regulatory structures…so that the region is not only open to more U.S. foreign direct investment, but that indigenous populations, indigenous innovators, [and] indigenous entrepreneurs can take advantage of the investment environments to drive economic growth throughout the region" (Wong 2018). To America, creating good rules facilitating investment between itself and regional economies will not only heighten trade and investment, but bolster prosperity for all involved, resulting in a win-win situation.[9] As far as infrastructure/connectivity is concerned, the administration wants to promote good governance, especially in regards to the facilitation of high-quality infrastructure, best-value or cost-effective connectivity projects, and sustainable development (*NSS* 2017, 47).

Additionally, the Trump administration wants to forge and strengthen partnerships with regional participants and institutions to identify, finance, and implement fiscally sound connectivity projects.[10] This is unsurprising, as Washington is increasingly disturbed by China's BRI and its state-driven model of infrastructure development, which is usually geared towards reaching the financier's strategic aspirations.[11] To delineate this point, a 2017 U.S.-China Economic and Security Review Commission's report raised concerns about China's role in connectivity projects in mainland Southeast Asia, where the country has "capitalized on regional countries' infrastructure needs"

(U.S.-China Economic and Security Review Commission 2017, 11). Beijing's financial support has enabled it to get access to key strategic locations such as ports, thereby tipping the policy behavior of these ASEAN members in its favor. The report also questioned Beijing's business model in terms of transparency, environmental impact, and its effect on the livelihood of local people, e.g., "Chinese dams on the Mekong River threaten the food security of 60 million people, creating significant stability risks" (U.S.-China Economic and Security Review Commission 2017, 11). Therefore, the United States plans to develop financing institutions and work with like-minded entities in order to promote a developmental model encouraging private sector involvement and economic growth, as well as bring tangible benefits to local societies.[12]

America's connectivity pursuit is reflected in Trump's remarks at the 2017 APEC CEO Summit in Vietnam. The president pledged to support multilateral financing institutions, namely the "World Bank and the Asian Development Bank[,] to direct their efforts toward high-quality infrastructure investment that promotes economic growth[,]" and to reform the American "development finance institutions so that they better incentivize private sector investment in…[regional] economies, and provide strong alternatives to state-directed initiatives that come with many strings attached" (Trump 2017b).

Following his rhetoric, work is being undertaken. The bipartisan BUILD Act of 2018, aimed at consolidating American development financial authorities, was introduced

> *The BUILD Act will heighten Washington's connectivity assistance in the Indo-Pacific region*

to Congress on March 1, 2018. The House and Senate passed the legislation in September and October 2018 by a vote of 398–23 and 93–6, respectively. Trump signed the act into law on October 5, 2018. The BUILD Act will heighten Washington's connectivity assistance in the Indo-Pacific region. First, it will undertake the reform of American development finance institutions by creating the U.S. International Development Finance Corporation (IDFC). This new entity will "assume the activities of the Overseas Private Investment Corporation (OPIC), USAID's Development Credit Authority, USAID's Enterprise

Funds, and USAID's Office of Private Capital and Microenterprise" (U.S. Senate Committee on Foreign Relations 2018). Also, the bill grants IDFC "the ability to make equity investment, a doubling of the contingent liability ceiling to $60 billion, and an extended operating authority" (Ingram 2018). Besides this reform, Washington has been engaging other regional governments to jointly pursue infrastructure building in the Indo-Pacific. For example, America, Japan, India, and Australia are collectively examining ways to set up financing schemes to mend the connectivity gaps in the region (*Reuters* 2018a). In addition, U.S. and Japanese agencies signed a memorandum of understanding (MOU) to provide high-quality energy infrastructure for emerging Indo-Pacific clients (JBIC 2017).

2. Reception of Regional States to the U.S. Indo-Pacific Strategy

Like the United States, other regional states have coined their own Indo-Pacific strategy. So far, the Trump administration's vision of a "Free and Open Indo-Pacific" has been met with positive reactions from certain regional states, as they realize what President Trump has in mind. The Japanese version of its own "Free and Open Indo-Pacific" strategy, which can be teased out from Japanese Prime Minister Shinzo Abe's speech "The Confluence of the Two Seas" to the Indian Parliament in 2007, emphasizes the importance of "maintaining and strengthening a free and open maritime order based on the rules of law in this region…and making the seas…a 'global commons' that brings stability and prosperity to all countries."[13] India, which has incorporated the Indo-Pacific concept since 2012 to showcase New Delhi as a regional power, envisions the region as free, open, rules-based, and inclusive (Government of India 2018). Furthermore, Australia's *2017 Foreign Policy White Paper* depicts the country as "determined to realise a secure, open and prosperous Indo–Pacific" (Government of Australia 2017). The U.S. policy also aligns with Australia's interest in maintaining the balance of power in the region, as outlined in the latter's white paper. In addition, Indonesia's concept of the Indo-Pacific collaboration rests on the principles of openness, transparency, inclusiveness, and of upholding international law (Marsudi 2018).

Several foreign actors were delighted to learn that the United States sees the importance of small- and medium-sized actors and multilateral institutions shaping regional governance architectures.[14] Such a stance was reflected in the *NSS* document (*NSS* 2017, 46) and Secretary Wong's remark that

> [considering] the strategic logic of an organization like ASEAN, it's an opportunity for small[-] and medium-sized countries to band together, use their collective weight, [and to] work in consensus in order to balance larger powers in the region and throughout the world… [Thus, the American] corollary policy…is to invest or continue to invest in ASEAN, continue to invest in APEC, to ensure that these regional organizations which convene the nations of the entire Indo-Pacific are committed to the principles [Washington considers to create] strategic…[and] economic benefits" (Wong 2018).

Notably, this American policy situates Southeast Asia in the middle, or at the "heart" of, the Indo-Pacific region, paving the way for the latter's elevated role in altering the future development of regional architecture. It also alludes to Washington's desire to leverage regional mechanisms to further deepen economic collaboration between itself and regional parties.

Nevertheless, many Asian policymakers cast doubt on exactly how the United States will implement its plans to advance economic cooperation in the three areas—trade, investment, and infrastructure—it has pledged.[15] The question then becomes: What are the actual programs Washington wants to create and/or advance to help it accomplish such collaboration? The jury is still out on that. In addition, recent U.S. moves have left regional governments uncertain about the former's seriousness about fostering a "Free and Open Indo-Pacific."

Washington desires to leverage regional mechanisms to further deepen economic collaboration between itself and regional parties

For instance, when launching a trade war with China, Trump has ignored the fact that Southeast Asian inputs are incorporated into the latter's exports to the United States. And in April 2018, the administration threatened to withdraw a special tariff treatment for Indonesia (Beo Da Costa 2018). Moreover, some regional states perceive that the

U.S. vow to leverage regional platforms such as ASEAN and APEC to execute its Indo-Pacific strategy seem empty, as little concrete action has followed that pledge.[16] To summarize, although more articulation is needed, the U.S. Indo-Pacific strategy in its current form, with America's continued engagement with regional players and multilateral institutions, is to some degree reassuring to Indo-Pacific actors.[17] As a result, this partly explains why this American policy has been welcomed by regional governments.

Washington's plans to engage the region in the realm of connectivity/infrastructure have met with positive feedback

It is worth noting that the degree of reception to the Trump strategy varies across economic areas. Washington's plans to engage the region in the realm of connectivity/infrastructure have met with more positive feedback when compared to the strategy's other two aspects. Several Indo-Pacific stakeholders applauded America's agenda to supply infrastructure alternatives to the existing options to help fulfill their needs.[18] According to the Asian Development Bank (ADB) (ADB 2017), there exists a huge financing gap in developing Asia. The zone would need more than $1.7 trillion annually from 2016–2030 to meet connectivity/infrastructure needs, but multilateral development banks were able to fund only 2.5 percent of that demand. This deficit partly contributed to the delayed implementation of regional connectivity programs. For example, the Trans-ASEAN Gas Pipeline program, purposed to connect Southeast Asia's gas exporters to consumers, and the ASEAN Power Grid initiative, aimed at combining national energy markets into a regional market, were less than 50 percent completed by 2015 (Pitakdumrongkit 2018a).

In addition, the U.S. plan syncs well with power balancing concerns of some regional states.[19] Craving for connectivity improvement notwithstanding, the Indo-Pacific stakeholders do not blindly scramble for external support. Regional states increasingly realize the risk of a sovereignty trade-off, especially when they overwhelmingly rely on certain donors and financiers over others. Assistance, financial and otherwise, given by other actors often comes with "strings attached," which may someday enable donors to gain leverage over recipients, altering international dynamics.[20] Since the 99-year lease of Sri

Lanka's Hambantota Port to China and the 414-kilometer Vientiane-Kunming high-speed railway project between China and Laos were announced, sovereignty concerns heightened. Regarding the Sino-Laos high-speed rail program, observers raised questions about the project's commercial viability, Laos' ability to pay back loans, and the issue of expropriated land (Hutt 2018). To elaborate, the scheme is worth US$6 billion, which is about half the state's 2016 GDP of US$13.7 billion. It was also reported that Beijing reached a deal with Laos to take the latter's land for 50 meters on each side of the track (Janviroj 2017). Such news not only makes Indo-Pacific nations wary of accepting economic development assistance from powerful foreign entities, it also fuels pushback against assistance and compels them to tread more cautiously. For instance, India has halted the progress of the Bangladesh-China-India-Myanmar (BCIM) initiative—originated in 1999—as it was roped under China's BRI banner (Singh, Sinderpal 2018). In Cambodia, public outcry concerning the lack of transparency and environmental impact of BRI projects has recently intensified (Moss 2018). After Cambodian authorities approved a plan to build the largest airport in Southeast Asia—in Kandal Province—with support from the China Development Bank, Cambodia's civil society reprimanded the program's debt sustainability (Kimsay and O'Byrne 2018).

While some Indo-Pacific participants pushed back against their donors and external influence, others chose to diversify. For instance, Indonesia's Jokowi administration, despite awarding China a Jakarta-Bandung high-speed railway project in 2015, tried to navigate among big powers (Moss 2018). "Concerned about appearing to be in China's pocket, senior government officials are looking to South Korean and Japanese investors to provide more balance." The Indonesian officer in the article reportedly encouraged Japanese firms to bid for the state's oil and gas blocks in 2017 (McBeth 2017). Moreover, at the time of this writing, the 350-kilometer Singapore-Kuala Lumpur high-speed train project is currently up for open bidding and it is expected there will be a face-off among European, Chinese, and Japanese companies for the contract award (Mazumdaru 2018). The urge for regional states to diversify partly explains why the U.S.-ASEAN Smart Cities Partnership launched at the U.S.-ASEAN Summit in November 2018 was greeted with enthusiasm by ASEAN countries. The initiative is aimed at augmenting Southeast Asian digital economies (Widakuswara 2018). Particular Indo-Pacific states are keen to see the United States provide additional infrastructure assistance, as this would widen their range of possible connectivity programs, allowing the states to undertake power balancing to serve their own interests.

Nevertheless, certain regional stakeholders are skeptical about the extent to which America could implement its connectivity policy. As of 2016, U.S. corporations had $1.7 trillion in savings, $1.2 trillion of which was parked overseas (Platt 2016). While this money could be used to invest in connectivity projects in the Indo-Pacific, the American private sector has little appetite for such investment due to the region's poor investment grade credit ratings and scarce availability of bankable projects (Bhattacharyay, Kawai, and Nag 2012). One study found that 55-65 percent of the connectivity projects in Asia are unbankable without support from governments or multilateral financing institutions (Marsh & McLennan Companies 2017). Moreover, an American authority noted that infrastructure financing by U.S. firms in Asia has declined since the Asian Financial Crisis of 1997–1998, as American resources were diverted from the region to fulfill rising connectivity demands in the United States. Additionally, the U.S. business model renders its public officers less able to effectively rally the private sector to invest where they desire. This makes regional states question Washington's ability to harness private finance to contribute to connectivity projects in the Indo-Pacific. Furthermore, many regional actors doubt U.S. ability to tailor connectivity programs to fit the needs of a region so diverse, as different Indo-Pacific economies are at dissimilar stages of development.[21]

In the area of investment, Asian nations welcomed the principles laid out by the Trump administration, especially increased private sector investment, which encourage investment projects that can boost entrepreneurship and innovation due to the aligning of economic goals. Nevertheless, they are unsure of the U.S. policy measures themselves, as not much is known about the rules and regulations to be crafted to promote or uphold the above principles. Frequently discussed questions by Indo-Pacific policymakers include: Will Washington be willing to work together with several Asian actors to jointly develop rules to bolster good investment governance architectures, or will the United States unilaterally create rules and impose them on other regional stakeholders? [22]

Additionally, Indo-Pacific stakeholders are worried about the implications of recent American actions on the future of U.S.-Asia investment flows. For instance, in August 2018, Trump signed into law the Foreign Investment Risk Review Modernization Act of 2018 (FIRRMA), which expands the authority of the Committee on Foreign Investment in the United States (CFIUS). CFIUS is an interagency committee mandated to review transactions that can lead to foreign acquisitions of American businesses to determine their effects on American national security.

In investment, will Washington be willing to work together with several Asian actors?

As a result, CFIUS has become more vigilant in preventing foreign acquisition of sensitive American technological innovation. This was reflected in a pilot program, which began on November 10, allowing the agency to review certain foreign investments in U.S. businesses in 27 sectors including aviation, semiconductors, and telecommunications. This means that such investments enabling foreign investors to gain "access to non-public information or afford power to nominate a board member or make other substantial decisions" must be subject to review under CFIUS. CFIUS will determine whether it approves the transaction within 30 days or trigger a fuller investigation (Bartz 2018). While this program shows CFIUS' new power, some questions remain, such as whether the agency would be granted power to oversee additional types of transactions, including "investments where a foreign company would not necessarily gain control of a U.S. firm…[such as]…joint ventures between U.S. and foreign companies, minority stake investments and transactions near military bases or U.S. government facilities" (Lane 2018). Moreover, whether such review would be under the jurisdiction of CFIUS or the export regulations of the Commerce Department is still up for debate (McQueen 2018). This effort to reform CFIUS sparked angst among not only American but Indo-Pacific investors. It is often argued that FIRRMA was mainly driven by Washington's desire to prevent Chinese takeovers of American firms and access to the former's technology (Cowan

2018). Nevertheless, Indo-Pacific companies are aware that their own investments might not be completely off the hook. A case in point is CFIUS blocking the March 2018 takeover attempt by Singapore-based Broadcom of American chipmaker Qualcomm (Granville 2018).

FIRRMA expands the scope of the agency's review to cover other industries such as real estate acquisitions near American military facilities (Hufbauer 2017). Additionally, one expert warned that the CFIUS reform could result in greater restrictions of U.S. outbound investment into the Indo-Pacific region. The reform could further undercut cross-border capital movements between American and regional economies.[23]

As far as trade is concerned, several Indo-Pacific participants don't believe the Trump administration will foster trade collaboration. From their perspective, America's current approach is a mercantilist, zero-sum framework in which balanced, bilateral trade is the primary goal. These regional stakeholders also doubt U.S. commitment in this area after Washington pulled out of TPP. This uncertainty, shared earlier by regional actors, changed to a feeling of disruption when Trump inked an MOU to impose 25 and 10 percent tariffs on imported steel and aluminium, respectively, in March 2018, which potentially hurt not only these industries but other sectors using these commodities as inputs.[24] This came just two months after the administration imposed tariffs on imports of solar panels and washing machines (Lynch 2018). At the time of this writing, these duties are still intact for most countries, including Canada and Mexico, the European Union (EU), and China (Dhue 2018). Tariff escalations and trade tensions resulted. For example, in April, China retaliated by slapping duties on the imports of 128 U.S. goods, ranging from pork to steel pipes (Buckley 2018). This was followed by a series of tariff increases by both sides, entangling them in a trade war (Martin and Bryan 2018; Mitchell et al. 2018; *Xinhuanet* 2018). However, the trade showdown was temporarily suspended when both

> *Some Indo-Pacific actors believe America's current approach is a mercantilist, zero-sum framework in which balanced, bilateral trade is the goal*

economies agreed on a 90-day truce at a sideline meeting at the G-20 Summit in Argentina on December 1, in which they agreed to sort out ways to resolve their conflicts, including those involving technology transfer and intellectual property rights (*BBC News* 2018; Breuninger and David 2018).

Although some experts argued that a Sino-U.S. trade war may eventually be avoided

At the G-20 Summit, China and the U.S. entered into a 90-day truce in their brewing trade war

due to the high cost for both sides,[25] this logic has not effectively quelled the angst held by Indo-Pacific parties for several reasons. First, Indo-Pacific nations acknowledge a shift in U.S. sentiment towards China. The majority of American think tanks and politicians share a position that China's noncompliance to international law warrants harsher American measures towards the latter. Capitol Hill's silence following the Trump administration's threat to slap tariffs on Chinese products is a case in point. No congressperson or senator came forward to chastise such action.[26] Another reason involves Trump's cabinet reshuffle. Larry Kudlow replacing Gary Cohn in March 2018 as the chief economic advisor has weakened the globalization faction within his cabinet.[27]

Also, stark differences between both sides await resolution. Washington demanded Beijing scrap its subsidies to industries under the "Made in China 2025" policy.[28] This initiative is a strategic plan unveiled by Chinese Premier Li Keqiang on May 2015, aimed at accomplishing Chinese competitiveness and prominence in 10 cutting-edge technological sectors such as aviation, robotics, and new energy vehicles. However, Chinese authorities insisted that "its industrial strategy was non-negotiable" (*South China Morning Post* 2018). Another event hinted that Beijing will not easily yield to Washington's demand. At a gathering to celebrate the 40th anniversary of China's Reform and Opening Up on December 18, President Xi Jinping voiced that "[n]o one is in a position to dictate to the Chinese people what should or should not be done" (*Channel NewsAsia* 2018).

Moreover, the 90-day ceasefire between the United States and China may not put an end to their trade war. Even though Beijing will make concessions until March 2019, it may not be able to fulfill the Trump administration's desires. China's purchase of a "very substantial" amount of agricultural, industrial, and energy goods from the United States is relatively easy, but the country might not be able to implement measures addressing its "unfair" trade practices to the extent that satisfies Washington within this 90-day timeframe, and hence a trade war may likely resume. As a result, Indo-Pacific stakeholders will proceed with caution in the new year (*BBC News* 2018).

Such a trade showdown does not bode well for Indo-Pacific states. As their economies are intertwined in cross-border production networks, they foresee themselves suffering from collateral damage. The America-China confrontation can to some degree hurt the intermediate goods exports among regional economies. Depending on the product, the latter distributes parts and components to China, which then assemble and ship the final products to the U.S. market. For instance, the components of iPhones from Asian economies are shipped to Foxconn factories located in Shenzhen, Chengdu, and other Chinese cities for final assembly, before exporting to the world. American tariffs on various Chinese products in the trade war will discourage the sales of regional goods. This will lead to a reduction of intermediate goods exports from other regional states. Moreover, such tariff dueling will likely significantly erode the competitiveness of smaller and medium enterprises (SMEs) more than large corporations, as the former are less able to relocate their factories and shift supply chains from one country to another.[29] SMEs are the backbone of several Asian economies. In the Indo-Pacific, they make up more than 90 percent of all businesses, contribute to one-third of the region's total export value, and provide two out of three private sector jobs.

As a result, the U.S.-Sino trade war will undermine regional state enterprises and economies (Yoshino and Taghizadeh-Hesary 2016). Some Indo-Pacific leaders have not been shy about voicing their concerns. Then-Australian Prime Minister Malcolm Turnbull remarked that nobody would win from a trade confrontation between the United States and China (*SBS News* 2018). Likewise, Singapore Prime Minister Lee Hsien Loong maintained that "unilateral tariffs are not the correct solution. A trade war between the United States and China...if [it] breaks out...will gravely undermine the rules-based multilateral system that has underpinned global prosperity since the end of World War II. Countries around the world, big and small, will be hurt" (Loong 2018).

Another source of Indo-Pacific agitation is the Trump administration's fixation on the goods trade deficit and focus on protecting U.S. intellectual property rights. This is reflected in the reports of the Office of the United States Trade Representative (USTR). The entity released a study listing several regional states having a goods trade surplus with Washington.[30] Also, USTR's 2017 Notorious Markets List, published in January 2018, named several online and physical markets in China, India, Indonesia, Pakistan, and Vietnam in which copyright infringement occurred. Moreover, the agency's 2018 Special 301 Report on Intellectual Property Rights released in April 2018 placed China, India, and Indonesia on the priority watch list, and Pakistan, Thailand, and Vietnam on the watch list. Such moves raised Asian policymakers' anxiety about the possibility of Washington's sanctions through tariffs or restrictions of Generalized System of Preferences (GSP) benefits.[31] Furthermore, as USTR launched Section 301 investigations on China and threatened to impose tariffs on the latter's exports, regional stakeholders viewed that the Super 301 mechanism could be used against them in the future (Section 301 of the Trade Act of 1974, as amended, gives the USTR broad authority to respond to a foreign nation's unfair trade practices.) Additionally, even though a U.S. State Department senior official assured that America's Indo-Pacific strategy is not aimed at containing China (Nelson 2017), Washington's recent harsh stance towards the latter tempted Asian policymakers to ponder if, in the future, they might be forced to choose between two great powers.[32]

3. Interactions between U.S. Indo-Pacific Strategy and Regional State Agendas

Interplay between the agendas of America and Indo-Pacific countries concerning regional economic building differ across issue areas. An obvious clash occurs between U.S. and Asian policies regarding ways to construct regional trade architectures. For the former, trade will be advanced via bilateral deals. According to President Trump's remarks at APEC's 2017 CEO Summit, Washington "will make bilateral trade agreements with any Indo-Pacific nation that wants to be our partner and that will abide by the principles of fair and reciprocal trade. What we will no longer do is enter into large agreements that tie our hands, surrender our sovereignty, and make meaningful enforcement practically impossible" (Trump 2017b). However, such insistence on bilateralism runs contrary to the trade regionalism approach of Asian states; these actors often favor multilateralism. This is partly because regional policymakers understand that bilateral trade negotiations usually set a big country (e.g., the United States) against a smaller one. This tends to increase the probability that big nations will pressure their smaller peers to agree on terms more favorable to the former.

Indo-Pacific actors largely oppose Washington's bilateral approach, partly accounting for why U.S. bilateralism has not received buy-ins from regional stakeholders. According to a Pew Research Center survey in June 2017, the majority of respondents in India, Indonesia, Japan, the Philippines, South Korea, and Vietnam opposed Trump's TPP withdrawal with a median of 66 percent. Asian diplomats are also dismayed that America lacks plans to foster a TPP-like overarching regional architecture covering not only multiple stakeholders, but other issues.[33] Some leaders were vocal about their disagreements towards America's approach. For example, Japanese Deputy Prime Minister Taro Aso declined the possibility of Tokyo entering into bilateral trade talks with Washington (Kihara 2018). While other Indo-Pacific players chose not to explicitly express their position, they nevertheless took a

> *Indo-Pacific actors do not want to negotiate bilateral deals with America, as doing so could put their countries at a disadvantage*

wait-and-see stance. Having watched NAFTA and KORUS renegotiations unfold, these actors suspect they will be strong-armed into making concessions or accepting contract terms overwhelmingly favoring the United States. Therefore, they do not want to negotiate bilateral deals with America, as doing so could put their countries at a disadvantage.[34]

Against this backdrop, what will likely be the future concerning regional trade architectures? The divergence of ideas and approaches between Washington and Indo-Pacific parties will persist. If cooperation is unattainable, the latter will continue to pursue regional economic institutional building for a few reasons. First, Asia's middle class—defined as comprising households with per capita incomes between $10 and $100 per person per day in 2005, in terms of purchasing power—is growing (Kharas 2017; Ernst & Young 2013). According to Homi Kharas of the Brookings Institution (Kharas 2017, 20), in 2022, Asians will emerge as the majority of individuals belonging to this income bracket. About 88 percent "of the next billion people in the middle class will be Asian." Such a rise will heighten future regional economic demand and become the catalyst for Indo-Pacific countries deepening their economic integration. A second factor is China. Chinese leaders recently reaffirmed their commitment to transform the state into a consumption- and service-driven economy over the next 10 years (GlobeNewswire 2018). Evidence points to regional economies being the main beneficiaries of this phenomenon. The region has witnessed a surge of Chinese tourists in

> *According to Homi Kharas, in 2022, Asians will emerge as the majority of individuals belonging to the middle class*

several Asian destinations. In the past decade, the number of Chinese tourists in Southeast Asia quadrupled (*The Economist* 2018). India witnessed a 15.6 percent increase in Chinese tourist arrivals from 2016–2017 (Singh, Swaran 2018), while Beijing surpassed New Zealand as Australia's biggest tourism market (Karaian 2018). In short, China's economic transformation will generate greater demands for goods and services from other Asian economies for years to come.

The efforts of governments in the Indo-Pacific to craft rules further deepening cross-border supply chains are reflected in CPTPP. This bloc is likely to expand because several economies, such as South Korea, Taiwan, Indonesia, and Thailand expressed their enthusiasm for joining (*The Japan Times* 2018b). Other attempts at deepening cross-border supply chains include the ongoing negotiation of RCEP. While RCEP may not be as ambitious as TPP (Wan 2018), this mega-trade deal's quality can be improved in the future if members agree to add a consulting mechanism allowing RCEP to have a regulatory framework upgrade. In this way, the multilateral arrangement's long-term values can be created. However, an involved mediator pointed to the fact that RCEP negotiation is a daunting task due to divergent levels of economic development, absence of prior bilateral deals between certain players such as China and India, India and New Zealand, and Japan and South Korea, and different preferences among parties (Robeniol 2018). These challenges may result in a bargaining stalemate. Even if RCEP talks collapse, trade regionalism is not entirely doomed. Rather, regional economies are still left with their existing trade treaties, namely ASEAN-China FTA (ACFTA), ASEAN-Japan Comprehensive Economic Partnership (AJCEP), ASEAN-Korea FTA (AKFTA), ASEAN-Australia-New Zealand FTA (AANZFTA), and ASEAN-India FTA (AIFTA). In the future, terms of these treaties can be improved to create better rules that enhance trade among members.

Unlike trade, Washington and Indo-Pacific national agendas concerning regional investment governance are not in direct contrast. However, with little coordination between them, their approaches could ultimately worsen the "investment noodle bowl" issue. To delineate this point, the United States and regional states usually make investment rules through bilateral international investment agreements (IIAs) and other contracts with investment provisions. As of May 10, 2018, America concluded 48 bilateral investment treaties (BITs), but only two with Indo-Pacific actors—Bangladesh and Sri Lanka. The United States also concluded bilateral trade deals that contained investment provisions with regional state economies South Korea (KORUS) and Laos (U.S.-Laos Trade Relations Agreement) (U.S. Department of State 2018a, 2018b; UNCTAD 2018).

Likewise, the common approach for Indo-Pacific players to bolster cross-border financial flows likens Washington's to a great degree. Illustratively, to date, they have concluded more than 1,000 BITs. Worldwide, about one-third of BITs have at least one Asian member as a contracting party. Moreover, these IIAs entail a relationship between regional and extra-regional parties. Indo-Pacific players tended to sign onto IIAs with their capital-intensive, capital-exporting partners, namely American and Western European economies (Chaisse and Hamanaka 2014).

While each regional investment initiative faces certain limitations lessening their ability to boost investment among U.S. and Indo-Pacific economies, a few exceptions to this trend deserve mentioning. First, we'll view the ASEAN Comprehensive Investment Agreement

(ACIA), signed by regional economic ministers in February 2009. ACIA merged two existing arrangements—the 1998 ASEAN investment area and the 1987 ASEAN investment guarantee agreement—to govern foreign direct investment into Southeast Asia under a single contract. Nevertheless, this framework targets only ASEAN and foreign ASEAN-based investors and investment institutions, meaning that foreign investors and institutions which are not based in Southeast Asia cannot benefit from the scheme. Another investment governance framework to look at is the RCEP FTA; this partnership's investment chapter can help foster transnational investment among its 16 members. However, these members constitute only a subset of countries in the Indo-Pacific. Additionally, the deal is still under negotiation and has faced several challenges, namely different levels of ambition among the negotiating parties and an absence of clear leadership, which could hurt the prospect of it coming to fruition by the end of 2019 as expected (Pitakdumrongkit 2018b).

In addition, TPP originally contained an investment chapter that could have augmented regional investment among the United States and its Indo-Pacific partners, such as Australia, Brunei, Japan, Malaysia, New Zealand, and Singapore. However, when Washington walked away in 2017, the pact resurrected as CPTPP, but this survived version suspended particular investment provisions, namely the investor-state dispute settlement (ISDS) clause. In cases which host governments breach a contract, the ISDS mechanism permits private entities to sue the former and bypass domestic courts, allowing them to take disputed cases to international arbitration tribunals. Without this provision, international investors may not feel that their investment is adequately protected. Consequently, because CPTPP lacks an ISDS, these investors may refrain from moving their capital to the Indo-Pacific area. In summation, while their approach to investment rule-making does not run in opposite directions, Washington and Indo-Pacific parties tend to commit "benign neglect" by paying little attention to the problem of IIA

> *Washington and Indo-Pacific parties tend to commit 'benign neglect' by paying little attention to the problem of IIA proliferation*

proliferation. While some regional investment governance arrangements attempt to address the issue, these arrangements face their own challenges as mentioned above. As the United Nations Conference on Trade and Development (UNCTAD)'s *World Investment Report 2011* precisely conveys, "[w]ith thousands of treaties, many on-going negotiations and multiple dispute-settlement mechanisms, today's IIA regime has come close to a point where it is too big and complex to handle for governments and investors alike" (UNCTAD 2011).

A central question then becomes: What would the future of regional investment governance architectures look like? One potential scenario is a fragmented investment governance system fueled by many IIAs and the persisting mutual ignorance by America and Indo-Pacific parties. This would have grave implications on the future of investment and trade characterized by cross-border supply chains. IIA proliferation begets a consistency problem, as different treaties may contain divergent rules, regulations, and legal interpretations which can, in the end, discourage investors from investing in multiple economies; this will undermine commerce among U.S. and regional economies. In other words, in order to facilitate transnational value chains, capital must first be allocated to establish and operate production facilities in several locations around the world. Hence, if these financial movements are hindered or disrupted by the "noodle bowl" issue, trade between America and its Indo-Pacific partners will be suppressed.

As far as connectivity/infrastructure governance is concerned, the interplay between U.S. and Indo-Pacific actors resembles that of the investment area. The region's infrastructure governance can be characterized by an alphabet soup of various connectivity schemes. Rules have been shaped by different donors, financiers, and frameworks with little coordination among them, making infrastructure investment more competitive than cooperative.[35] This leads to a governance problem. To delineate this point, conflicts may arise when the players involved attempt to link different connectivity projects (e.g., roads, railways) supported by dissimilar governance programs. These circumstances bring up a pressing issue: Which rules or standards (e.g., rail gauge width) are to be adopted? Although evidence indicates cooperation among different institutions, such as the cofinancing effort by the AIIB and ADB in projects in Bangladesh, Pakistan, Georgia, and India (*Reuters* 2018b), it is uncertain whether they will collaborate in the future. Different institutions usually have divergent visions, priorities, and practices concerning lending conditions, procurement procedures, and labor and environmental standards. Such dissimilarities can instigate conflicts in subsequent interactions. Also, less is known about how other entities would undertake cooperation. According to one public authority, while some regional players set up a discussion platform to boost coordination amongst themselves, no financial resources are allocated to fund concrete programs to materialize such collaboration.[36]

Besides uncoordinated physical infrastructure development, the region is tainted with an institutional connectivity problem. In fact, the development of "institutional infrastructure," namely, rules and regulations facilitating the flow of goods and services, often lags behind physical infrastructure building in several areas. This is mainly due to the fact that little effort has been put forth by regional actors to collectively make rules enhancing the facilitation of international logistics. This, hence, begets nonsynchronized regulatory frameworks hindering transnational goods and services transport. One study tracking the progress of the Greater Mekong Subregion (GMS)—a subregional cooperative program among China's Yunnan Province, Cambodia, Laos, Myanmar, Thailand, and Vietnam—revealed that while physical routes were completed, regulatory and administrative support was inadequate. This lack of support eventually became a barrier to the transit of goods and services. To illustrate, half of the time used to ship goods from Da Nang, Vietnam, to Tak Province, Thailand, was spent at customs and border crossings.

> *It's clear that nonalignment of rules and regulations hinder the transnational movement of goods and services*

"From a cost perspective, 42.6 [percent] of the door-to-door transport costs are collected at customs and border crossings. The amount is almost equivalent to the cost of physical transportation" (Banomyong 2010, 36). In addition, institutional logistical linkages between East and Southeast Asia are mostly absent. Take Myanmar, which is usually regarded as a country of land bridges between these two zones. According to a joint study by ADB and the Asian Development Bank

Institute (ADBI), there are no transit agreements between Myanmar and Thailand or Myanmar and India (ADBI 2015). Therefore, the future of regional connectivity governance architectures will likely be a fragmented one. There has been little coordination between different infrastructure providers and financial institutions. It is clear that nonalignment of rules and regulations hinder the transnational movement of goods and services.

4. Policy Recommendations

Notwithstanding the differences in approach to the development of regional economic governance architectures by Washington and Indo-Pacific nations, it is misguided to anticipate that economic regionalism will close off the United States to the area. Such a circumstance is highly unlikely, as regional economic architectures, namely ASEAN and APEC, have been built upon the principle of "open regionalism" (Bergsten 1997). Open regionalism is an outward-looking and liberal modality to regional economic integration in a sense that it embraces external parties in order to expand the networks of collaboration (Ravenhill 2000). For instance, the *AEC 2025* posits that ASEAN shall

> [d]evelop a more strategic and coherent approach towards external economic relations with a view to adopting a common position in regional and global economic fora…continue to review and improve ASEAN FTAs and CEPs to ensure that they remain modern, comprehensive, of high-quality and more responsive to the needs of businesses operating the production networks in ASEAN… [and]…enhance economic partnerships with non-FTA Dialogue Partners by upgrading and strengthening trade and investment work programmes/plans (ASEAN Secretariat 2015, 36).

Likewise, open regionalism is in the APEC spirit as seen in its official documents. For example, the 2001 APEC Leaders' Declaration refers to this bloc's unique modality, which is "based on the fundamental principles of voluntarism, consensus-building, combination of individual and collective actions, flexibility, comprehensiveness, and open regionalism, which has inspired and underpinned our successes" (APEC 2001). Thus, the door is still open for U.S. and Indo-Pacific players to foster—together—economic cooperation. The following are steps these policymakers can take to help them jointly advance regional economic governance architectures.

4.1. Immediately Pursue Collaboration in the Areas of Investment and Infrastructure/Connectivity

Given a clash in approaches concerning how to advance trade regionalism between Washington and Indo-Pacific participants, resources should first be invested in the deepening of international collaboration in the realms of investment and infrastructure/connectivity. At the time of this writing, the United States is taking a step in the right direction.

4.2. Advance Investment Cooperation via Capacity Training Programs and Investment Treaty Consolidation

The United States has great expertise in developing governance architecture of investment promotion, property registration, and contract enforcement. This has largely contributed to the nation's transparent and sophisticated financial system and worldwide recognition of the dollar as the international currency. Many economies resort to the greenback to settle transactions among themselves. Some countries have even undergone complete or partial dollarization by adopting the dollar for their domestic use. However, many regional players fare less well than America in terms of technical knowledge. Consequently, some have struggled to make good investment rules, and this partially accounts for their less developed financial systems. Hence, with its greater expertise, the United States can take the lead in sharing its knowledge, experiences, and best practices in the form of capacity training programs. Doing so will enrich Indo-Pacific stakeholder rule-making skills, enabling them to not only improve their own domestic financial systems, but advance regional mechanisms to better facilitate investment between American and regional economies; this knowledge can also be used or applied by regional stakeholders to enhance their regional frameworks. For example, ASEAN, China, Japan, and South Korea launched the Asian Bond Markets Initiative (ABMI) in December 2002 under the ASEAN-Plus-Three financial cooperation process. ABMI is aimed at developing local currency-denominated bond markets in order to better utilize regional savings and raise investment in Asia. However, the scheme's progress has been modest recently, partly due to members lacking expertise and experience in developing bond markets. Although ABMI is limited to ASEAN-Plus-Three members, in the future, this model of regional capital market building can be replicated in other parts of the Indo-Pacific if other actors have the know-how. In summary, Washington can leverage its financial adeptness to help provide capacity training for Indo-Pacific policymakers so that the latter can better implement investment rules and regulations at the national and regional levels, which in turn will increase investment among both regional and U.S. economies.

In cases where U.S. and regional participants want to make new investment treaties, joint effort should be made in helping address the fragmented Indo-Pacific investment governance system. There exists several ways to alleviate the IIA proliferation problem. For instance, UNCTAD's *World Investment Report 2017* outlines several solutions, such as treaty termination and suspension, in order to consolidate or manage different IIAs (UNCTAD 2017). Treaty termination can be achieved in different ways, such as aborting preexisting deals so that investment relationships are governed by a single contract. Article 21.7 of the Central America-Mexico FTA that abolished the Mexico-Nicaragua FTA is one example. Alternatively, the involved participants can suspend certain investment arrangements while keeping other agreements in force. The deactivation of the Switzerland–South Korea BIT (1971), when the Switzerland-Liechtenstein-Iceland-South Korea investment treaty (2005) took effect, is a case in point. When these options are not feasible, Washington and Indo-Pacific parties should work toward rule harmonization or the interoperationality of different investment regulations. Doing so can also help facilitate the movement of funds across borders.

4.3. Enhance Infrastructure/Connectivity Collaboration via BUILD Act, Joint Ventures, Public-Private Partnership, and Capacity Training

The United States should immediately implement the BUILD Act, as it will enhance the country's ability to more effectively roll out infrastructure finance instruments, hence elevating its role as a key player in Indo-Pacific connectivity development. Besides traditional connectivity construction, Washington and like-minded countries should stress the joint pursuit of e-infrastructure building due to rising regional demands. According to the World Bank, the 2016 Internet penetration rate in South Asia, and East Asia and Pacific was about 26 and 46 percent, respectively (World Bank 2016). Although ASEAN has the Initiative for ASEAN Integration (IAI) purposed to close development gaps among ASEAN parties, this scheme is limited to assist only Cambodia, Laos, Myanmar, and Vietnam (CLMV). As a result, the sockets in non-CLMV countries in need of e-connectivity cannot utilize IAI to fill their digital infrastructure gaps.

To enhance its role in regional infrastructure and finance development, the United States should immediately implement the BUILD Act

Contrary to criticism that the U.S. private sector's presence in the Indo-Pacific has diminished, America has been a key player in digital infrastructure construction. Its private conglomerates are at the forefront in this field. As Shambaugh (2018, 113) demonstrated, companies such as Amazon, Apple, eBay, Google, Oracle, Twitter, and Uber have actively supplied digital services and information technologies to their Indo-Pacific clients. The Trump administration is now unveiling initiatives to further tap into the technical capacities of these businesses. For instance, Secretary Pompeo announced in July 2018 that an initial $25 million investment would finance the Digital Connectivity and Cybersecurity Partnership aimed at augmenting regional state digital infrastructure through several means, including public-private partnership, to "catalyze American businesses to do what they do best" (Pompeo 2018). Additionally, via the Infrastructure Transaction and Assistance Network, the government will coordinate the involved agencies to assess projects, mobilize development finance, and supply technical assistance to Indo-Pacific nations.

Although these programs are laudable, the jury is still out on how they will be implemented to rally the U.S. private sector and boost their role in shaping Indo-Pacific digital connectivity. Therefore, it is suggested that U.S. authorities devise plans to coordinate among their related agencies, identify bankable projects, facilitate joint ventures between American and other state companies, and foster a more feasible environment for public-private partnership.

In addition to physical infrastructure building, American authorities and other entities can deliver capacity training to Indo-Pacific policymakers, enabling them to develop rules and regulations facilitating transnational logistics. For instance, the ADBI regularly trains Asian officials on how to develop economic corridors (ADBI 2018). Also, the U.S. Agency for International Development (USAID) has played a significant role in training Southeast Asian authorities to devise rules and regulations pertaining to trade facilitation, which ultimately led to a successful launch of the ASEAN Single Window (ASW) initiative in 2005. ASW is aimed at linking the national windows of all 10 ASEAN members to allow electronic data submission for cargo clearance, reducing the cost of doing business across these economies. Such training programs should be conducted with other Indo-Pacific countries to enable them to set up single windows in their respective subregions. Moreover, the capacity-building schemes should aim at tackling the fragmented connectivity governance marked by an alphabet soup of various frameworks. This can be done by organizing workshops on how to harmonize rules or boost the inter-operationality of different rules and regulations.

4.4. Push Forward Trade Cooperation via Formal and Informal Dialogue, with the Incorporation of Track 2 Networks into the Policymaking Process

Because Washington insists on fostering "free, fair, and reciprocal" trade, and "fair" is largely defined by a trade balance term, there exists little room for Asian participants, namely those running a trade surplus with America, to negotiate trade deals satisfying all involved. As mentioned, the U.S. and Indo-Pacific approach to trade regionalism is likely to continue to diverge. The former opts for bilateralism while the latter prefers multilateralism. Moreover, the prospect of the United States joining CPTPP is slim. According to one American government official, the tide is turning against this deal. The U.S. Congress censured several aspects of TPP/CPTPP, namely labor standards and safeguards and environmental protection, arguing that these elements could place American businesses at a disadvantage.

Capitol Hill also demanded these components be adequately resolved before the U.S. rejoins the pact.[37]

Against this backdrop, a pressing question is: How can America and regional states together foster regional trade governance architectures? Although these stakeholders may not be able to negotiate and conclude trade deals in the short term, they should maintain regular formal and informal dialogue on a bilateral and multilateral basis. Such communication is necessary because it not only helps the participants identify ways to advance trade collaboration, but also lessens the chance of misperceiving or misinterpreting one another's policies. With misperceptions and misinterpretations, economic tensions can escalate into a full-blown trade war, deteriorating U.S.-Asia commerce.

Multilateral discussions can be held at regional platforms, especially ASEAN and APEC forums, for the following reasons. First, these schemes aim at facilitating economic growth, trade, and investment cooperation in the region. ASEAN members are deepening regional economic integration by implementing policy measures outlined in the *AEC 2025*. The blueprint calls for: "(i) A Highly Integrated and Cohesive Economy; (ii) A Competitive, Innovative, and Dynamic ASEAN; (iii) Enhanced Connectivity and Sectoral Cooperation; (iv) A Resilient, Inclusive, People-Oriented, and People-Centred ASEAN; and (v) A Global ASEAN" (ASEAN Secretariat 2015, 1).

Likewise, APEC is purposed "to create greater prosperity for the people of the region by promoting balanced, inclusive, sustainable, innovative, and secure growth and by accelerating regional economic integration" (APEC 2018). Additionally, these forums embrace Track 2 networking—informal talks—as part of their decision-making. Illustratively, the "ASEAN Way"—a set of principles upheld by ASEAN members such as informal consultation—has been used to lessen international conflicts or collectively devise feasible solutions to address regional problems. APEC's discussions are often carried out in an open, nonbinding format which requires no treaty obligations. Such informality creates an atmosphere allowing those involved to be open and frank in exchanging concerns and test particular policy ideas before taking formal steps such as treaty formations. Contrary to criticism that these groupings are merely "talk shops," ASEAN and APEC act as incubators of ideas which later materialize as practical policies to advance economic architectures. The agreement on trade facilitation (often dubbed the "Bali Package") endorsed by the Ninth WTO Ministerial Conference in Bali, Indonesia, in 2013, is a case in point. The arrangement, which took effect on February 22, 2017, is aimed at "expediting the movement, release and clearance of goods, including goods in transit" in the region (WTO 2018). The agreement's origin can be traced back to APEC. The bloc's parties championed the idea of a trade facilitation pact and played a significant role in making it adoptable at the World Trade Organization level. In short, Washington and Indo-Pacific stakeholders can leverage the informality of these venues to foster open discussions and explore new or innovative means to push forward trade regionalism.

Besides intergovernmental organizations, Washington and regional states can leverage the expertise of think tanks and incorporate inputs from these Track 2 mechanisms into their policymaking process as well. American and Indo-Pacific officials should encourage an expansion of existing think tank networks such as the Network of East Asian Think-Tanks (NEAT) under the ASEAN-Plus-Three structure, and the Asian Think Tanks Network (ATTN) supported by ADB. NEAT was established in 2003 as a Track 2 unit providing policy inputs to the ASEAN-Plus-Three cooperation process. Founded in 2013, the main objective of ATTN is boosting "systematic knowledge sharing among member think tanks, specifically on development experiences and policy lessons…[and augmenting] the think tank's capacity to generate knowledge or provide policy advice on its domain" (ATTN 2018). The membership of both groups can be enlarged to include think tanks from America and other countries. Utilizing Track 2 networking is crucial, as it helps explore certain issues too sensitive to be discussed at intergovernmental or Track 1 (official government-to-government) platforms. Therefore, discourse among think tanks can enable countries to jointly examine economic issues and craft innovative solutions to problems. These recommendations can be forwarded to public officers to assist the latter's policy formulation.

Informal talks: Track 2 networking helps explore certain issues too sensitive to be discussed at intergovernmental or Track 1 platforms

4.5. Foster Inter-Institutional Cooperation: Inter-Bloc Dialogue Encouragement

One effective way to advance Indo-Pacific economic cooperation is creating an overarching governance architecture which not only encompasses all Indo-Pacific stakeholders, but also covers collaboration in several economic aspects. This framework can act as a venue for the economies involved to discuss economic matters and challenges, and collectively devise policy actions to tackle such issues. For example, American and Indo-Pacific authorities can utilize this platform to adopt certain policy stances and approaches more compatible with each other. However, creating such a comprehensive umbrella organization may not be feasible at present, as doing so would require substantive resource allocation.

While on July 18, Secretary Pompeo announced that America will support regional institutions such as ASEAN, APEC, and IORA, there has been no concrete action made by this administration to encourage dialogue among existing regional bodies. Thus, this paper suggests the United States and regional governments consider strengthening inter-institutional ties by initiating dialogue among different cooperative blocs. For example, conversations should be promoted among the Bay of Bengal Initiative for Multi-Sectoral Technical and Economic Cooperation (BIMSTEC), IORA, ASEAN, and APEC, as these entities have several Indo-Pacific nations as members and focus on bolstering international economic collaboration. Formed in June 1997, the main goal of BIMSTEC is "to harness shared and accelerated growth through mutual cooperation" via sector-driven collaboration such as trade and investment, transport and communication, energy, and tourism (BIMSTEC 2018). Its current members are Bangladesh, Bhutan, India, Myanmar, Nepal, Sri Lanka, and Thailand. IORA was created in March 1997 as an intergovernmental organization with a focus on strengthening "economic dialogue and regional cooperation to promote sustainable growth and balanced development for a prosperous Indian Ocean Rim." The entity features 21 members, including Australia, Bangladesh, India, Indonesia, Malaysia, Singapore, Sri Lanka, and Thailand. America is also among its dialogue partners (IORA 2018).

Such inter-institutional communications are crucial as they increase the likelihood that these parties identify specific areas for cooperation. Doing so can lead to venues in which regional states can voice their concerns and exchange views on regional economic governance. Moreover, increased interactions through inter-bloc dialogue could breed trust among these stakeholders, paving a way for the future creation of an Indo-Pacific-wide economic grouping.

Conclusion

This study has discussed the impact of the Trump administration's Indo-Pacific strategy on regional economic governance. The text has shown that this strategy's economic components cover three areas: trade, investment, and infrastructure development. While the strategy's trade elements are likely to clash with policies promoted by regional states, U.S. and regional government approaches to investment and infrastructure are not diametrically opposed. However, both American and Indo-Pacific nations have largely ignored the issue of fragmented governance systems in investment and infrastructure realms, which, with overlapping rules and regulations, can worsen the situation and hamper the ease of doing cross-border business. The paper has also provided policy recommendations to enhance collaboration among the United States and Indo-Pacific countries in these three areas.

At the time of this writing, the Trump administration is rolling out programs as outlined by Secretary Pompeo in July 2018. These will be among the first batch of initiatives to test the impact of the U.S. Indo-Pacific strategy on regional economic governance. Interested scholars should assess the effectiveness of these schemes after their implementation and view how they interact with other initiatives advanced by other states and international organizations. Doing so can help us arrive at a more comprehensive picture of the effects of America's Indo-Pacific strategy on regional economic governance.

Endnotes

1. Interview with former Obama White House staffer by author, Washington D.C., April 9, 2018.

2. Interview with U.S. State Department official by author, Washington D.C., April 19, 2018.

3. Interview with Rear Admiral Michael McDevitt, U.S. Navy (retired) by author, Washington D.C., April 18, 2018.

4. See note 1.

5. See note 1.

6. Interview with professor Robert Sutter, The George Washington University Elliott School of International Affairs, by author, Washington D.C., April 2, 2018.

7. See note 2.

8. See note 1.

9. See note 1.

10. See note 2.

11. Interview with former U.S. congressional staffer by author, Washington D.C., April 17, 2018.

12. See note 1.

13. Interview with Kentaro Sonoura, special advisor to Japanese Prime Minister Abe Shinzo, regarding Abe's keynote speech at the 2014 Shangri-la Dialogue in Singapore, May 4, 2018.

14. Interview with Asian diplomats by author, Washington D.C., April 18, 2018.

15. See note 14.

16. Interview with former U.S. State Department officer by author, Washington D.C., April 25, 2018.

17. Interview with American academic by author, Washington D.C., May 1, 2018.

18. See note 14.

19. Interview with Asian policymaker by author, Washington, D.C., May 24, 2018.

20. See note 16.

21. Interview with U.S. think tank scholar by author, Washington, D.C., April 5, 2018.

22. See note 14.

23. See note 21.

24. See note 11.

25. See note 21.

26. Interview with former U.S. Defense Department authority by author, Washington, D.C., April 23, 2018.

27. See note 6.

28. The phrase "Made in China" is largely a misnomer because it ignores the fact that a significant amount of parts and components of electronic and high-end manufactured products are sourced from other Asian economies.

29. See note 11.

30. Interview with U.S. think tank scholar by author, Washington, D.C., April 2, 2018.

31. See note 21.

32. Interview with maritime security expert by author, Washington, D.C., April 24, 2018.

33. See note 14.

34. See note 11.

35. Interview with the chair of Southeast Asia Program Advisory Board, Center of International and Strategic Studies (CSIS) by author, Washington, D.C., April 16, 2018.

36. Interview with U.S. State Department official by author, Washington, D.C., June 11, 2018.

37. Interview with U.S. Congressional staffer by author, Washington, D.C., May 3, 2018.

Bibliography

Asia-Pacific Economic Cooperation (APEC). 1993. "Leaders' Declaration." APEC Ministerial Meeting, Blake Island, Seattle, November 20, 1993. https://www.apec.org/Meeting-Papers/Leaders-Declarations/1993/1993_aelm.

———.1994. "Leaders' Declaration." APEC Ministerial Meeting, Bogor, Indonesia, November 16, 1994. https://www.apec./Meeting-Papers/Leaders-Declarations//1994_aelm.

Asia-Pacific Economic Cooperation (APEC). 2001. "Leaders' Declaration." APEC Ministerial Meeting, Shanghai, October 21, 2001. https://www.apec.org/MeetingPapers/Leaders-Declarations/2001/2001_aelm.

———. 2018. "About APEC." Accessed on June 12, 2018, from https://www.apec.org/About-Us/About-APEC .

Association of Southeast Asian Nations (ASEAN). 2015. *ASEAN Economic Community Blueprint 2025* (*AEC 2025*). Jakarta: ASEAN Secretariat. https://www.asean.org/storage/2016/03/AECBP_2025r_FINAL.pdf.

Asian Development Bank (ADB). 2017. "Asia Infrastructure Needs Exceed $1.7 Trillion Per Year, Double Previous Estimates," news release, February 28, 2017. https://www.adb.org/news/asia-infrastructure-needs-exceed-17-trillion-year-double-viousestimates.

Asian Development Bank Institute (ADBI). 2015. *Connecting South Asia and Southeast Asia*. Tokyo: Asian Development Bank Institute. https://www.adb.org/sites/default/files/publication/159083/adbi-connecting-south-asia.pdf.

———. 2018. "Year in Review 2017: Capacity Building and Training." https://www.adb.org/adbi/year-in-review/capacity-building-training.

Asian Infrastructure Investment Bank (AIIB). 2018. "Who We Are." Accessed on August 28, 2018, from https://www.aiib.org/en/about-aiib/index.html.

ADB–Asian Think Tanks Network (ATTN). 2018. "About Us." Accessed on June 15, 2018, from http://www.adb-asianthinktanks.org/aboutus.

Ayres, Alyssa. 2017. "Want A Free And Open 'Indo-Pacific'? Get India Into APEC." *Forbes*, November 10, 2017. https://www.forbes.com/sites/alyssaayres/2017/11/10/a-freeand-open-indo-pacific-get-india-into-apec/#209846dc5b4c.

Banomyong, Ruth. 2010. "Benchmarking Economic Corridors logistics performance: a GMS border crossing observation." *World Customs Journal* 4, no. 1: 29–38. http://worldcustomsjournal.org/Archives/Volume%20 4%2C%20Number%201%20(Mar%202010)/05%20Banomyong.pdf.

Bartz, Diane. 2018. "Tighter US foreign investment rules aimed at China start in November." *Reuters*, October 10, 2018. https://www.reuters.com/article/us-usa-tradesecurity/tighter-us-foreign-investment-rules-aimed-at-china-start-in-november-idUSKCN1MK1IC.

Bay of Bengal Initiative for Multi-Sectoral Technical and Economic Cooperation (BIMSTEC). 2018. "About BIMSTEC." Accessed on June 15, 2018, from https://bimstec.org/?page_id=189.

BBC News. 2018. "US-China trade war: Deal agreed to suspend new trade tariffs." December 2, 2018. https://www.bbc.com/news/world-latin-america-46413196.

Beo Da Costa, Agustinus. 2018. "Indonesia lobbies US to maintain special tariff treatment." *Reuters*, August 5, 2018. https://in.reuters.com/article/us-usa-trade-indonesia/indonesialobbiesu-s-to-special-tariff-treatment-idINKBN1KQ04P.

Bergsten, Fred. 1997. "Open Regionalism." Working Paper 97-3. Peterson Institute for International Economics, January 1997. https://piie.com/publications/workingpapers/open-regionalism.

Bhattacharyay, Biswa Nath, Masahiro Kawai, and Rajat Nag. 2012. *Infrastructure for Asian Connectivity*. Cheltenham, UK: Edward Elgar Publishing Limited (Asian Development Bank Institute and Asian Development Bank). https://www.adb.org/sites/default/files/publication/159325/adbi-infra-asian-connectivity.pdf.

Biermann, Frank, Philipp Pattberg, Harro van Asselt, and Fariborz Zelli. 2009. "The Fragmentation of Global Governance Architectures: A Framework for Analysis." *Global Environmental Politics* 9, no. 4 (November 2009): 14–40. https://www.mit.org/doi/10.1162/glep.2009.9.4.14.

Breuninger, Kevin, and Javier David. 2018. "US will hold off on raising China tariffs to 25% as Trump and Xi agree to a 90-day trade truce." *CNBC Politics*, December 1; updated December 3, 2018. https://www.cnbc.com/2018/12/01/us-china-additional-tariffs-after-january-1-report.html.

Buckley, Chris. 2018. "China Slaps Tariffs on 128 US Products, Including Wine, Pork and Pipes." *The New York Times*, April 1, 2018. https://www.nytimes.com/2018/04/01/world/asia/china-tariffs-united-states.html.

Chaisse, Julien, and Shintaro Hamanaka. 2014. *The Investment Version of the Asian Noodle Bowl: The Proliferation of International Investment Agreements*. ADB Working Paper Series on Regional Economic Integration, no. 128 (April). Manilla: ADB. http://hdl.handle.net/11540/4189.

Channel NewsAsia. 2017. "US defends use of 'Indo-Pacific' over 'Asia-Pacific', says it reflects India's rise." November 6, 2017. https://www.channelnewsasia.com/news/defends-use-of-indo-pacific-over-asia-pacific-says-it-9380420.

———. 2018. "No one can 'dictate' to China what it should do: Xi Jinping." December 18, 2018. https://www.channelnewsasia.com/news/asia/china-xi-one-can-dictate-what-it-should-do-11041910.

Clarke, Michael, and Anthony Ricketts. 2017. "Donald Trump and American foreign policy: The return of the Jacksonian tradition." *Comparative Strategy* 36, no. 4 (November 1): 366–379. https://doi.org/10.1080/01495933.2017.1361210.

Cowan, Richard. 2018. "Republican senators, president to discuss anti-China measure at White House." *Reuters*, June 5, 2018. https://www.reuters.com/article/us-usa-cfius-/republican-senators-president-to-discuss-anti-china-measure-at-white-house-idUSKCN1J12Q5.

Dhue, Stephanie. 2018. "Steel and aluminum tariffs remain a headache despite Trump's trade deal with Mexico and Canada." *CNBC Politics*, November 30; updated December, 1 2018. https://www.cnbc.com/2018/11/30/steel-aluminum-tariffs-remain-even-signs-new-nafta-deal.html.

Douglas, Walter. 2018. "New Zealand, the United States, and the Indo-Pacific." Remarks by Walter Douglas, Deputy Assistant Secretary, Bureau of East Asian and Pacific Affairs. Auckland, March 26, 2018. https://www.state.gov/p/eap/rls/rm/2018/03/279557.htm.

East-West Center. 2013. "Asia Matters for America/America Matters for Asia." https://asiamattersforamerica.org/uploads/publications/2013-Asia-Matters-for-America.pdf.

———. 2017. "India Matters for America/America Matters for India." https://asiamattersforamerica.org/uploads/publications/2017-India-Matters-for-America.pdf.

The Economist. 2018. "East Asia has the world's fastest growing tourist industry." April 12, 2018. https://www.economist.com/asia/2018/04/12/east-asia-has-the-worlds-fastest-tourist-industry.

Ernst & Young. 2013. "Hitting the sweet spot: The growth of the middle class in emerging markets." http://www.ey.com/Publication/vwLUAssets/Hitting_the_sweet_spot/%24FILE/Hitting_the_sweet_spot.pdf.

Feaver, Peter. 2009. "What is grand strategy and why do we need it?" *Foreign Policy*, April 8, 2009. https://foreignpolicy.com/2009/04/08/what-is-grand-strategyandwhy-do-we-need-it.

Futurenautics. 2013. *Global Marine Trends 2030*. http://www.futurenautics.com/wp-content/uploads/2013/10/GlobalMarineTrends2030Report.pdf

Global Times. 2017. "China maps out 'Belt and Road' with action plan." May 4, 2017. http://www.globaltimes.cn/content/1045361.shtml.

GlobeNewswire. 2018. "China Pushes Towards a Consumption-Driven Growth Model as the Country Renews Its Commitment to Quality of Growth and Technology," press release, January 25, 2018. https://globenewswire.com/news-release/2018/01/25/1305168/0/en/China-Pushes-Towards-a-Consumption-Driven-Growth-Model-as-the-Country-Renews-Its-Commitment-to-Quality-of-Growth-and-Technology.html.

Government of Australia. 2017. *2017 Foreign Policy White Paper*. Barton ACT: Government of Australia. https://www.fpwhitepaper.gov.au.

Government of Canada. 2018. "Overview and benefits of the CPTPP." Accessed on August 28, 2018, from http://international.gc.ca/trade-commerce/agreements-accords-/acc/cptpp-ptpgp/overview-apercu.aspx?lang=eng.

Government of India. 2018. "Prime Minister's Keynote Address at Shangri[-]La Dialogue." Singapore, June 1, **2018**. https://www.mea.gov.in/Speeches-Statements.htm?dtl/29943/Prime+Ministers+Keynote+Address+at+Shangri+La+Dialogue+June+01+2018.

Granville, Kevin. 2018. "Cfius, Powerful and Unseen, Is a Gatekeeper on Major Deals." *The New York Times*, March 5, 2018. https://www.nytimes.com/2018/03/05/business/what-is-.html.

Green, Michael, and Andrew Shearer. 2012. "Defining US Indian Ocean Strategy." *The Washington Quarterly 35*, no. 2: 175–89. https://doi.org/10.1080/0163660X.2012..

Grossman, Marc. 2018. "Energizing Strategies for the Indo-Pacific." *YaleGlobal Online*, April 3, 2018. https://yaleglobal.yale.edu/content/energizing-strategies-indo-pacific.

Gupta, Anubhav. 2017. "Trump should champion India for Asia-Pacific economic pact." *The Hill*, November 9, 2017. https://thehill.com/opinion/international/359551trump-should-champion-india-for-asia-economic-pact.

Hanson, Victor Davis. 2017. "A Jacksonian Manifesto." *America Greatness*, December 18, 2017. https://amgreatness.com/2017/12/18/a-jacksonian-.

Hufbauer, Gary Clyde. 2017. "Has the US gone too far in revamping its foreign investment regime?" East Asia Forum, December 15, 2017. http://www.eastasiaforum.org/2017/12/15/has-the-us-gone-too-far-in-revamping-its-foreign-investment-regime.

Hutt, David. 2018. "Laos on a fast track to a China debt trap." *Asia Times*, March 28, 2018.

Ingram, George. 2018. "Building a robust US development finance institution." Brookings Institution, March 29, 2018. https://www.brookings.edu/blog/future-development/2018/03/29/building-a-robust-us-development-finance-institution.

Indian Ocean Rim Association (IORA). 2018. "IORA at a glance." Accessed on June 15, 2018, from https://www.iora.int/media/8249/iora-at-a-glance.pdf.

Jack, Ian. 2018. "India has 600 million young people – and they're set to change our world." *The Guardian Opinion*, January 13, 2018. https://www.theguardian.com//2018/jan/13/india-600-million-young-people-world-cities-internet.

Janviroj, Pana. 2017. "Laos; from land locked to land linked." *The Nation*, September 12, 2017. http://www.nationmultimedia.com/detail/big_read/30326442.

The Japan Times. 2018a. "16 Asia-Pacific nations eye 2019 conclusion of RCEP trade deal after delay." November 14, 2018. https://www.japantimes.co.jp/news/2018/11/14/business/16-asia-pacific-nations-eye-2019-conclusion-rcep-trade-deal-delay/#.XDudYreWw5s.

———. 2018b. "CPTPP: A victory for reason in trade." March 13, 2018. https://www.japantimes.co.jp/opinion/2018/03/13/editorials/cptpp-victory-reason-trade/#.XDugGreWw5s.

Japan Bank for International Cooperation (JBIC). 2017. "JBIC Signs MOU with OPIC of the US," press release, November 8, 2017. https://www.jbic.go.jp/en/information/press/press-2017/1108-58390.html.

Jozuka, Emiko. 2017. "TPP vs RCEP? Trade deals explained." *CNN*, January 26, 2017. https://www.cnn.com/2017/01/24/asia/tpp-rcep-nafta-explained/index.html.

Karaian, Jason. 2018. "More tourists in Australia now come from China than New Zealand." *Quartz*, April 21, 2018. https://qz.com/1258898/chinese-tourists-in-australia-now-outnumber-visitors-from-new-zealand.

Kharas, Homi. 2017. "The Unprecedented Expansion of the Global Middle Class: An Update." Global Economy & Development Working Paper 100, Brookings Institution, February 2017. https://www.brookings.edu/wp-content/uploads/2017/02/global_20170228_global-middle-class.pdf.

Kihara, Leika. 2018. "Japan's Aso rules out bilateral trade deal with US." *Reuters*, March 28, 2018. https://www.reuters.com/article/us-japan-us-trade/japans-aso-rules-out-trade-deal-with-u-s-idUSKBN1H50B7.

Kimsay, Hor, and Brendan O'Byrne. 2018. "Government plans one of world's biggest airports in Kanda." *The Phnom Penh Post*, January 15, 2018. https://www.phnompenhpost.com/business/government-plans-one-worlds-biggest-airports-kandal.

Lane, Sylvan. 2018. "Alarmed by foreign deals, lawmakers eye new review powers." *The Hill*, May 2, 2018. http://thehill.com/policy/finance/385749-alarmed-by-foreign-deals-lawmakers-eye-new-review-powers.

Loong, Lee Hsien. 2018. "Singapore's prime minister: Nobody wants a trade war." *The Washington Post*, April 18, 2018. https://www.washingtonpost.com/opinions/singapores-prime-minister-nobody-wants-a-trade-war/2018/04/18/64d9fa30-431e-11e8-ad8f-27a8c409298b_story.html?utm_term=.addc3e5c9700.

Lynch, David. 2018. "Trump imposes tariffs on solar panels and washing machines in first major trade action of 2018." *The Washington Post*, January 22, 2018. https://www.washingtonpost.com/news/wonk/wp/2018/01/22/trump-imposes-tariffs-on-solar-panels-and-washing-machines-in-first-major-trade-action/?utm_term=.af0aebe69c66.

Marsh & McLennan Companies, Asia Pacific Risk Center. 2017. *Closing the financing gap: Infrastructure Project Bankability in Asia*. New York: Marsh & McLennan Companies. https://www.marsh.com/ph/insights/research/closing-the-financing-gap-infrastructure-project-bankability-in-asia.html.

Marsudi, Retno. 2018. "[Full text] Indonesia: Partner for peace, security, prosperity." *The Jakarta Post*, January 11, 2018. https://www.thejakartapost.com/academia//01/10/full-text-indonesia-partner-for-peace-security-prosperity.html.

Martin, Will, and Bob Bryan. 2018. "China hits back at Trump with tariffs on $60 billion of US goods." *Business Insider*, September 18, 2018. https://www.businessinsider.com/trade-war-china-to-retaliate-to-fresh-trumps-200-billion-tariffs-2018-9.

Mazumdaru, Srinivas. 2018. "Europe faces China, Japan in high-speed rail battle in Asia." *Deutsche Welle*, February 14, 2018. https://www.dw.com/en/europe-faces-china-in-speed-rail-battle-in-asia/a-42589008.

McBeth, John. 2017. "Is Indonesia's Widodo in China's pocket?" *Asia Times*, December 11, 2017.

McQueen, MP. 2018. "CFIUS Reform Is Likely, but 'Joint Venture' Provision in Play, Lawyers Say." *The National Law Journal*, June 4, 2018. https://www.law.com/nationallawjournal/2018/06/04/cfius-reform-is-likely-but-joint-venture-provision-in-play-lawyers-say.

Mistry, Dinshaw. 2016. *Aligning Unevenly: India and the United States*. Policy Studies No. 74. Honolulu: East-West Center. https://www.eastwestcenter.org/system/tdf/private/ps074.pdf?file=1&type=node&id=35623.

Mitchell, Tom, Emily Feng, and Xinning Liu. 2018. "China retaliates against new US tariffs as trade war escalates." *Financial Times*, September 18. 2018. https://www.ft.com/content/a12104b6-bb14-11e8-94b2-17176fbf93f5.

Moss, Daniel. 2018. "Indonesia's Jokowi counts on populism." *The Myanmar Times*, May 8, 2018. https://www.mmtimes.com/news/indonesias-jokowi-counts-populism.html.

National Defense Strategy (NDS). 2018. "Summary of the 2018 National Defense Strategy of the United States of America: *Sharpening the American Military's Competitive Edge*." Department of Defense, January 19, 2018. https://dod.defense.gov/Portals/1/Documents/pubs/2018-National-Defense-Strategy-Summary.pdf.

National Security Strategy of the United States of America (*NSS*). 2017. Washington, D.C.: The White House. https://www.whitehouse.gov/wp-content/uploads/2017/12/NSS-Final-12-18-2017-0905.pdf.

Nelson, Louis. 2017. "In Asia, Trump keeps talking about Indo-Pacific." *Politico*, November 7, 2017. https://www.politico.com/story/2017/11/07/trump-asia-indo-pacific-.

Office of the United States Trade Representative (USTR). 2018. *2018 Trade Policy Agenda and 2017 Annual Report of the President of the United States on the Trade Agreements Program*. Washington, D.C.: USTR. https://ustr.gov/sites/default/files/files/Press/Reports/2018/AR/2018%20Annual%20Report%20FINAL.PDF.

Pence, Mike. 2018. "Remarks by Vice President Pence at the 2018 APEC CEO Summit."Port Moresby, Papua New Guinea, November 16, 2018. https://www.whitehouse./briefings-statements/remarks-vice-president-pence-2018-apec-ceo-summit-port-moresby-papua-new-guinea.

Pitakdumrongkit, Kaewkamol. 2018a. "Southeast Asia and China's Maritime Silk Road."Conference paper. 5th Annual RSIS-CNA Workshop on East Asian Maritime Issues: Indo-Pacific Maritime Issues: Connectivity, Balance and Cooperation. Singapore, March 7–8, 2018.

———. 2018b. "RCEP: Another Missed Deadline." RSIS Commentary 189, November 14, 2018. https://www.rsis.edu.sg/rsis-publication/cms/rcep-another-misseddeadline/#.bVVKiM-.

Platt, Eric. 2016. "US companies' cash pile hits $1.7tn." *Financial Times*, May 20, 2016. https://www.ft.com/content/368ef430-1e24-11e6-a7bc-ee846770ec15.

Pompeo, Mike. 2018. "Remarks on 'America's Indo-Pacific Economic Vision'" by Secretary of State Mike Pompeo. Washington, D.C., July 30, 2018. https://www.state./secretary/remarks//07/284722.htm.

Ravenhill, John. 2000. "APEC adrift: implications for economic regionalism in Asia and the Pacific." *The Pacific Review 13*, no. 2: 319–333. https://doi.org/10.1080/095127400363613.

Reuters. 2018a. "Australia, US, India and Japan in talks to establish Belt and Road alternative: report." February 18, 2018. https://www.reuters.com/article/china-beltandroad-quad/australia-u-s-india-and-japan-in-talks-to-establish-belt-and-road-alternative-report-idUSKCN1G20WG.

———. 2018b. "ADB, China-backed AIIB to co-finance more projects this year." January 12, 2018. https://www.reuters.com/article/adb-asia-aiib/adb-chinabacked-aiibtocofinance-more-projects-this-year-idUSL4N1P72UI.

Robeniol, Anna. 2018. "The 17th ASEAN Lecture on the Regional Comprehensive Economic Partnership (RCEP) – Progress, Outstanding Issues and Outlook." ISEAS-Yusof Ishak Institute, Singapore, June 8.

Samaranayake, Nilanthi. 2012. *The Long Littoral Project: Bay of Bengal*. Arlington, VA:CNA. https://www.cna.org/cna_files/pdf/irp-2012u-final.pdf.

SBS News. 2018. "No one wins from a China-US Trade war, Turnbull says." March, 23 2018. https://www.sbs.com.au/news/no-one-wins-from-a-china-us-trade-warturnbullsays.

Shambaugh, David. 2018. "US-China Rivalry in Southeast Asia: Power Shift or Competitive Coexistence?" *International Security 42*, no. 4 (Spring 2018): 85–127. https://.org/10./_a_00314.

Singh, Sinderpal. 2018a. "South Asia and the Maritime Silk Road: Far From Plain-sailing." RSIS Commentary 57, March 28, 2018. https://www.rsis.edu.sg/rsis-publication/rsis/-south-asia-and-the-maritime-silk-road-far-from-plain-sailing/#.XEkiClVKiM8.

Singh, Swaran. 2018b. "Rising tide of Chinese tourists visiting India." *China Plus*, January 22, 2018. http://chinaplus.cri.cn/opinion/oped-blog/23/20180122/81048.html.

South China Morning Post. 2018. "China may send 'firefighter' Wang Qishan to negotiate with US on trade." May 13, 2018. https://www.scmp.com/news/china/diplomacydefence/article/2145873/china-may-send-firefighter-wang-qishan-negotiate-us.

Trump, Donald. 2017a. "Remarks by President Trump on the Administration's National Security Strategy." Washington, D.C., December 18, 2017. https://www.whitehouse.gov/briefings-/remarks-president-trump-administrations-nationalsecuritystrategy.

———. 2017b. "Remarks by President Trump at APEC CEO Summit." Da Nang, Vietnam, November 10, 2017. https://www.whitehouse.gov/briefings-statements/remarkspresident-trump-apec-ceo-summit-da-nang-vietnam.

United Nations Conference on Trade and Development (UNCTAD). 2011. *World Investment Report 2011*. New York and Geneva: United Nations. https://unctad.org/en/PublicationsLibrary/wir2011_en.pdf.

———. 2016. *Review of Maritime Transport 2016*. New York and Geneva: United Nations. https://unctad.org/en/PublicationsLibrary/rmt2016_en.pdf.

———. 2017. *World Investment Report 2017*. New York and Geneva: United Nations. http://unctad.org/en/PublicationsLibrary/wir2017_en.pdf.

———. 2018. "The United States of America." Investment Policy Hub database. Accessed on May 10, 2018, from http://investmentpolicyhub.unctad.org/IIA/CountryIris/223#iiaInnerMenu.

United States Energy Information Administration (US EIA). 2017. "Almost 40% of global liquefied natural gas trade moves through the South China Sea." November 2, 2017. https://www.eia.gov/todayinenergy/detail.php?id=33592.

United States Department of State (U.S. Department of State). 2018a. "United States Bilateral Investment Treaties."Accessed on May 10, 2018, from https://www.state.gov/e/eb/ifd/bit/117402.htm.

———.2018b. "Advancing a Free and Open Indo-Pacific Region." November 18, 2018. https://www.state.gov/r/pa/prs/ps/2018/11/287433.htm.

U.S.-China Economic and Security Review Commission. 2017. "2017 Report to Congress of the U.S.-China Economic and Security Review Commission: Executive Summary and Recommendations." November. https://www.uscc.gov/sites/default/files/annua_reports/2017%20Executive%20Summary%20and%20Recommendations_1.pdf.

United States Census Bureau (U.S. Census Bureau). 2018a. "Trade in Goods with Asia." Business & Industry, Foreign Trade. Accessed on September 12, 2018, from https://www.census.gov/foreign-trade/balance/c0016.html.

———. 2018b. "Top Trading Partners - July 2018." Accessed on September 12, 2018, from https://www.census.gov/foreign-trade/statistics/highlights/top/top1807yr.html.

United States Senate Committee on Foreign Relations (U.S. Senate Committee on Foreign Relations). 2018. "Corker, Coons Introduce Bill to Modernize US Approach to Development Finance," press release, February 27, 2018. https://www.foreign.senate.gov/press/chair/release/corker-coons-introduce-bill-to-modernize-us-approach-to-development-finance.

Wan, Dandan. 2018. "Asia's Trade Spaghetti Bowl -TPP11 and RCEP." EU-Asia Centre, April 6, 2018. http://www.eu-asiacentre.eu/pub_details.php?pub_id=236.

Widakuswara, Patsy. 2018. "Pence Announces US-ASEAN 'Smart Cities Partnership.'" *Voice of America*, November 15, 2018. https://www.voanews.com/a/us-asean-smart-cities-partnership-/4659652.html.

Wong, Alex. 2018. "Briefing on The Indo-Pacific Strategy." Remarks by Deputy Assistant Secretary Alex Wong. Washington, D.C., April 2, 2018. https://www.state.gov/r/pa/prs/ps/2018/04/.htm.

World Bank. 2017. "Individuals using the Internet (% of population)." Accessed June 12, 2018, from https://data.worldbank.org/indicator/IT.NET. USER.ZS?view=map.

World Trade Organization (WTO). 2018. "Trade facilitation." Accessed June 12, 2018, from https://www.wto.org/english/tratop_e/tradfa_e/tradfa_e.htm.

Xinhuanet. 2018. "China announces anti-dumping measures on US sorghum." April 17, 2018. http://www.xinhuanet.com/english/2018-04/17/c_137117475.htm.

Yoshino, Naoyuki, and Farhad Taghizadeh-Hesary. 2016. "Major Challenges Facing Small and Medium-sized Enterprises in Asia and Solutions for Mitigating Them." ADBI Working Paper 564, April 2016. https://www.adb.org/sites/default/files//182532/adbi-wp564.pdf.

Acknowledgments

This project was supported by the East-West Center's Asia Studies Fellowship program. I wish to thank Dr. Satu Limaye, director, and the staff at the East-West Center in the Washington, D.C. for their kind support. Also, I would like to thank anonymous reviewers whose useful comments enabled me to significantly improve my paper.

www.ingramcontent.com/pod-product-compliance
Lightning Source LLC
Chambersburg PA
CBHW050530210326
41520CB00012B/2507